THIS BOOK WAS
PURCHASED WITH FUNDS FROM THE
HOLIDAY RUN & WALK SPONSORED BY THE
KIWANIS CLUB OF THE DELTA AND PG&E

LIVING GREEN

FOOD

Information and projects to reduce your environmental footprint

Marshall Cavendish
Benchmark
New York

Helen Whittaker

This edition first published in 2012 in the United States of America by
Marshall Cavendish Benchmark
An imprint of Marshall Cavendish Corporation

Website: www.marshallcavendish.us

This publication represents the opinions and views of the author based on Helen Whittaker's personal experience, knowledge, and research. The information in this book serves as a general guide only. The author and publisher have used their best efforts in preparing this book and disclaim liability rising directly and indirectly from the use and application of this book.

Other Marshall Cavendish Offices:
Marshall Cavendish Ltd. 5th Floor, 32-38 Saffron Hill, London EC1N 8FH, UK • Marshall Cavendish International (Asia) Private Limited, 1 New Industrial Road, Singapore 536196 • Marshall Cavendish International (Thailand) Co Ltd. 253 Asoke, 12th Flr, Sukhumvit 21 Road, Klongtoey Nua, Wattana, Bangkok 10110, Thailand • Marshall Cavendish (Malaysia) Sdn Bhd, Times Subang, Lot 46, Subang Hi-Tech Industrial Park, Batu Tiga, 40000 Shah Alam, Selangor Darul Ehsan, Malaysia

Marshall Cavendish is a trademark of Times Publishing Limited

All websites were available and accurate when this book was sent to press.

Library of Congress Cataloging-in-Publication Data

Whittaker, Helen.
   Food / Helen Whittaker
   p. cm. — (Living Green)
   Includes index.
   Summary: "Discusses how food growth and consumption impact the environment and what you can do to be more eco-conscious"—Provided by publisher.
   ISBN 978-1-60870-574-0
   1. Sustainable agriculture—Juvenile literature. 2. Food habits—Juvenile literature. 3. Environmentalism—Juvenile literature. I. Title.
   S494.5.S86W485 2012
630—dc22
                         2010044339

First published in 2011 by
MACMILLAN EDUCATION AUSTRALIA PTY LTD
15–19 Claremont Street, South Yarra 3141

Visit our website at www.macmillan.com.au or go directly to www.macmillanlibrary.com.au

Associated companies and representatives throughout the world.

Publisher: Carmel Heron
Commissioning Editor: Niki Horin
Managing Editor: Vanessa Lanaway
Editor: Georgina Garner
Proofreader: Helena Newton
Designer: Julie Thompson
Page layout: Julie Thompson
Photo researcher: Claire Armstrong (management: Debbie Gallagher)
Illustrators: Nives Porcellato and Andrew Craig (11); Cat MacInnes (all other illustrations)
Production Controller: Vanessa Johnson

Printed in China

Acknowledgments
The author and the publisher are grateful to the following for permission to reproduce copyright material:

Front cover photograph: Girl in fridge courtesy of Getty Images/Ray Pietro. Front and back cover illustrations by Cat MacInnes

Photographs courtesy of: Getty Images/Alexandra Grablewski, 26, /JupiterImages, 18, /Lester Lefkowitz, 9 (top); iStockphoto.com/cjp, 16, /Creativestock, 24, /Greg da Silva, 31, /ParkerDeen, 15, /James Whittaker, 3, 22; Shutterstock/Akaiser, (environment icons, throughout), /Vadim Balantsev, 13 (bottom left), /Katrina Brown, 4, 32, /Ivan Cholakov Gostock-dot-net, 10 (aeroplane), /Frontpage, 6 (bottom), /Natali Glado, 14 (bottom), /gsmad, 30 (middle), /Péter Gudella, 10 (truck), /khz, 8 (bottom), /Fedor Kondratenko, 12 (bottom), /Laenz, (eco icons, throughout), /Olivier Le Queinec, 12 (top), /mmaxer, 30 (top), /Monkey Business Images, 5, 8 (top), 13 (bottom right), /Martin Muránsky, 13 (middle), /naluwan, 10 (top), /Orange Line Media, 13 (top), /Denis Pepin, 28, /Mark R, 7 (bottom), /Rafael Ramirez Lee, 10 (ship), /Sever180, 14 (top), /Andrey Shadrin, 6 (top), /Kenneth Sponsler, 10 (train), /tepic, 20, J van der Wolf, 7 (top), 9 (bottom left), /Vishnevskiy Vasily, 21, /Jaren Jai Wicklund, 9 (bottom right), /Ye, (recycle logos, throughout), /Jin Young Lee, 30 (bottom).

Please note
At the time of printing, the Internet addresses appearing in this book were correct. Owing to the dynamic nature of the Internet, however, we cannot guarantee that all these addresses will remain correct.

1 3 5 6 4 2

Contents

Protect your veggies from hungry pests! page 20

Glossary Words

When a word is printed in **bold**, you can look up its meaning in the Glossary on page 31.

Grow your own veggies at home! page 18

Living Green

Living green means choosing to care for the **environment** by living in a sustainable way.

Living Sustainably

Living sustainably means living in a way that protects Earth. Someone who lives sustainably avoids damaging the environment or wasting resources so that Earth can continue to provide a home for people in the future.

You and your friends can change your habits and behavior to help Earth. Living green makes sense!

How Our Actions Affect the Environment

Human activities use up Earth's **natural resources** and damage the environment. Some natural resources are **renewable**, such as wind and water, and some are **nonrenewable**, such as the **fossil fuels coal** and **oil**.

As the world's population grows, people are using more water, which creates water shortages, and are causing water **pollution**. We are using more nonrenewable resources too, which are usually mined from the earth and then burned, causing **habitat** destruction and air pollution. People cannot continue to live and act the way they do now—this way of life is unsustainable.

What Is an Environmental Footprint?

A person's environmental footprint describes how much damage that person does to the environment and how quickly the person uses up Earth's resources. A person who protects the environment and does not waste resources has a light environmental footprint. A person who pollutes the environment and wastes resources has a heavy environmental footprint.

Food

The foods we choose to eat have an impact on the environment. Understanding these environmental effects can help us eat "greener" and live more sustainably!

How Food Affects the Environment

Food has an environmental impact at every stage of the journey, from the field to your plate. The chemicals used in farming can harm the environment. Transporting, storing, and cooking food uses a lot of energy. Most of this energy is generated by burning fossil fuels, which uses up natural resources, destroys habitats, pollutes the air, and releases **carbon dioxide**, a **greenhouse gas** that contributes to **global warming**.

Where to Next?

• To find out how the growing, processing, packaging, transporting, and cooking of food affects the environment, go to the "Background Briefing" section on page 6.
• To try out fun projects that will help you reduce your environmental footprint, go to the "Living Green Projects" section on page 16.

How Does Cooking Frozen Peas Affect the Environment?

The peas that you eat have usually traveled a long way! They have had many negative effects on the environment.

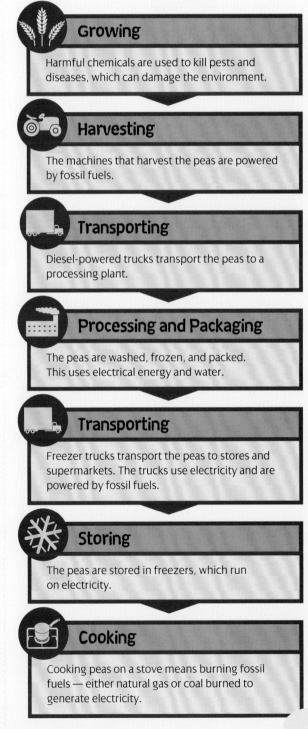

Growing

Harmful chemicals are used to kill pests and diseases, which can damage the environment.

Harvesting

The machines that harvest the peas are powered by fossil fuels.

Transporting

Diesel-powered trucks transport the peas to a processing plant.

Processing and Packaging

The peas are washed, frozen, and packed. This uses electrical energy and water.

Transporting

Freezer trucks transport the peas to stores and supermarkets. The trucks use electricity and are powered by fossil fuels.

Storing

The peas are stored in freezers, which run on electricity.

Cooking

Cooking peas on a stove means burning fossil fuels — either natural gas or coal burned to generate electricity.

Growing Food

Most of the food you eat is not grown in a sustainable way. Growing it does a lot of damage to the environment.

The Environmental Impacts of Growing Food

Across the world, land is cleared to sow crops and so animals can graze. Freshwater is used to water these crops and to provide water for animals. Clearing land destroys habitats and, in dry areas, crops need to be watered, which uses up a natural resource. Most farmers use chemicals to **fertilize** the land and to kill pests and weeds and prevent diseases. These chemicals have negative effects on the environment.

Land-clearing for Farming

Every year large areas of natural vegetation are cut down to make way for new farmland. This destroys natural habitats and contributes to global warming. The world demand for food is growing as the world's population grows, so more and more land is being cleared.

Irrigation

In dry areas, crops are **irrigated**, which can lead to water shortages. Irrigation also causes salts in the soil to come to the surface. Over time, the soil may become too salty for plants to grow.

Clearing natural habitats for farming harms Earth. This land in the Amazon region of South America was once covered in rain forest, but it has now been cleared for cattle-grazing.

Agricultural Chemicals

Agricultural chemicals damage the soil, harm wildlife, and wash into rivers and streams, where they pollute the water supply and destroy habitats.

Environmental Effects of Agricultural Chemicals

Type of Chemical	Purpose	Environmental Effects
Fertilizers	To add **nutrients** to the soil to make crops grow better	Fertilizers washed into waterways can create an **algal bloom**, which may kill plants and animals that live in the water.
Insecticides	To kill insects that might eat the crop	Insecticides also kill insects that help some plants to reproduce.
Herbicides	To kill weeds that might crowd out the crop	Weeds provide food for animals, so destroying them removes the animals' food.
Fungicides	To kill **fungi** that might reduce the amount of food the crop produces	Fungi turn dead plant matter into soil and are an important part of the environment.

ECO FACT

Eating meat has a huge environmental impact. The process of producing meat—from clearing land for grazing to the gases that cattle and sheep release—produces more greenhouse gases each year than all the world's cars, planes, trains, and airplanes combined.

An algal bloom can harm animals such as ducks. A bloom occurs when the amount of algae in a waterway grows extremely quickly, often after fertilizers are washed into it.

Processing and Packaging food

Once food has been harvested, it is usually taken to a factory to be processed and packaged so that it can be sold. Processing and packaging have impacts on the environment.

The Environmental Impacts of Processing and Packaging Food

Some of the foods you eat, such as kiwis and avocados, come in their own natural packaging! Adding more packaging just creates a lot of extra garbage.

Processing and packaging food uses lots of energy and natural resources, and also creates a lot of garbage. Processing involves changing food to make it more convenient to use, for example by cleaning it, cutting it up, or precooking it. Most processed foods need to be packaged to keep them safe to eat and to make them easy to transport.

Processing Food

Food processing uses up natural resources and energy. Most of this energy is generated by burning fossil fuels, which harms the environment and is not sustainable.

Milk pasteurization is a process that makes milk safer to drink and helps keep it fresh for longer. There are many steps in this process and most of these steps use a lot of electrical energy.

ECO FACT

Pasteurization was invented in 1864, by the French scientist Louis Pasteur, as a way to stop beer and wine from going sour. Today, many foods and liquids are pasteurized.

The Pasteurization Process

This flowchart shows the main steps involved in pasteurizing milk.

Cows are milked on a dairy farm.

The milk is stored in a refrigerated container.

The milk is transported to the dairy factory in a refrigerated truck.

The milk is forced between metal plates or through pipes heated on the outside by hot water. It is heated to 162°F (72°C) for 15 seconds.

The milk is cooled quickly to 39°F (4°C).

The milk is packed in bottles and cartons that are free from **bacteria**.

The milk is transported to supermarkets and stores in refrigerated trucks.

The milk must be stored at or below 39°F (4°C).

Milk doesn't come straight from a cow! Factories use a lot of electricity to heat the milk, cool the milk, and pack the milk that will eventually end up in your refrigerator.

Packaging Food

Packaging food is a waste of resources. If the packaging is not **recycled**, it contributes to the world's growing mountains of **landfill**. Most processed foods need to be packaged, but lots of unprocessed foods do not.

Transporting Food

The food you eat has to be transported from where it is produced to where it will be sold. Whichever way food is transported — whether by truck, train, ship, or airplane — it has an effect on the environment.

The Environmental Impacts of Transporting Food

Transporting food thousands of miles from one continent to another is not sustainable. Ships, planes, and trucks burn a lot of fossil fuels.

Which Transportation Has the Least Impact?

Trucks, trains, ships, and airplanes all burn fossil fuels, which pollute the air with carbon dioxide. Some vehicles release more carbon dioxide than others. Carbon dioxide is linked to global warming, so the more carbon dioxide a vehicle produces, the more it harms the environment. Air transport is by far the most polluting and least sustainable way to transport food.

Transportation Vehicles and How Much Carbon Dioxide They Release

Transportation vehicle	Carbon dioxide (ounces/grams) released when carrying 1 ton (1 tonne) of food over 0.5 miles (1 kilometer)
Train	1.4–1.7 ounces (39–48 grams)
Ship	1.5–2 ounces (40–60 grams)
Truck	7–10 ounces (207–280 grams)
Airplane	40–75 ounces (1,160–2,150 grams)

Where Does Our Food Come From?

Most countries produce only a fraction of the food they need. The rest is **imported** from all over the world. Some countries make more food than they need, but they **export** some types of food and import other types.

Where the different foods in your supermarket come from depends on the country you live in and what time of year it is. For example, oranges are a winter fruit, so if you live in the United States and you buy an orange in the summer, it has probably been brought all the way from a country below the equator, where it is the winter.

ECO FACT

The distance that food travels from where it is grown to where it is eaten is called its "food miles." Food that is produced and eaten locally has low food miles, and food that is transported between two countries has high food miles. Food miles account for just one part of a food's environmental impact and its overall sustainability.

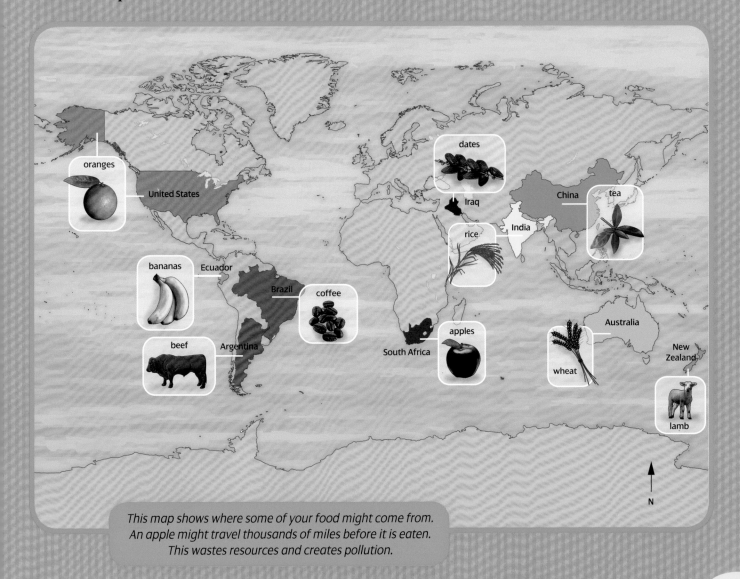

This map shows where some of your food might come from. An apple might travel thousands of miles before it is eaten. This wastes resources and creates pollution.

Storing and Cooking Food

Once food arrives at a supermarket, it continues to have an environmental impact. Cooking food and certain ways of storing food use energy.

The Environmental Impacts of Storing and Cooking Food

Some foods need to be stored in a refrigerator or freezer. Keeping these foods cool on the way to supermarkets, in the supermarket, and in your home uses lots of electricity, and this has a negative impact on the environment. Cooking the food uses up natural resources, such as wood and fossil fuels.

Storing food in a refrigerator has an environmental impact because it uses a lot of electrical energy. The larger the refrigerator, the more energy it uses.

Storing Food in a Refrigerator or Freezer

Food stored in a refrigerator or freezer keeps fresh for longer because low temperatures slow down the growth of bacteria and fungi, which make food go bad. Refrigerators and freezers are powered by electricity, most of which is generated by burning fossil fuels.

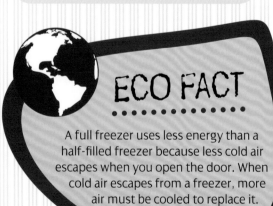

ECO FACT

A full freezer uses less energy than a half-filled freezer because less cold air escapes when you open the door. When cold air escapes from a freezer, more air must be cooled to replace it. This uses energy.

Cooking Food

The way food is cooked affects the environment. Cooking methods such as microwaving, barbecuing, and cooking on an electric stove pollute the air, either directly or indirectly. They also have other harmful effects on the environment.

The Environmental Impacts of Cooking Food

Cooking Method	How It Works	Environmental Impacts
Using an electric stove	Runs on electricity. Most electricity is generated by burning fossil fuels.	Fossil fuels are nonrenewable. They harm the environment and contribute to global warming.
Using a microwave oven		
Using a gas stove	Burns gas, which is a fossil fuel	
Barbecuing	Burns wood or charcoal (the charred remains of wood)	Burning creates air pollution. When trees are cut down for wood or charcoal, they are not always replanted. Trees help the environment by absorbing carbon dioxide.
Using a wood stove	Burns wood	

What Can You Do?

There are lots of things you can do to reduce the environmental impact of the food you eat. Eating more sustainably doesn't have to be boring. In fact, it can be delicious!

Green Tips for Choosing Food

Choose foods that:

✓ are grown locally and do not need to travel far

✓ are in season where you live. These foods are less likely to have traveled long distances, which means they are often a bargain, too!

✓ are **organic**, which means that chemical fertilizers and **pesticides** have not been used on them

Avoid:

✗ foods that have a lot of packaging

✗ eating a lot of meat, because producing meat releases greenhouse gases

✗ eating fish that are **overfished**

What is Overfishing?

Overfishing is when fish are caught faster than they can breed, causing fish numbers to sink to very low levels. Overfishing can change the balance of the environment and cause some types of fish and animals to become extinct. A type of fish that is threatened by overfishing is bluefin tuna.

Green Tips for Reducing Food Waste

Three ways to reduce food waste are:

✔ grow some of your own food (see pages 16–23)

✔ only buy the amount of food you need

✔ recycle leftover food by turning it into compost

Green Tips for Finding Sustainable Food

Good places to find sustainable food are:

✔ local farmers' markets

✔ the organic aisle of your local supermarket

✔ bulk food bins in whole-food stores, which do not use unnecessary packaging

✔ in your own backyard. Food that you grow yourself is sure to be local, seasonal, organic, and very, very fresh

At a local farmers' market, you can buy food that is locally grown and possibly organic.

Living Green Ratings and Green Tips

Pages 16–29 are filled with fun projects that will help you grow your own food, use local products, and protect Earth from waste and pollution.

Each project is given its own Living Green star rating— from zero to five—as a measurement of how much the project lightens your environmental footprint.

Some projects give Green Tips telling you how you can improve the project's Living Green rating even more.

Green Tip

To improve the Living Green rating, make the strap from an old belt or a bicycle inner tube.

On each project spread, look for the Living Green rating. Five stars is the highest—and greenest—rating!

Living Green Rating
★ ★ ★ ★ ★

★ ★ ★	★ ★ ★ ★	★ ★ ★ ★ ★
A three-star project will teach you about an issue and explain how you are wasting natural resources or causing pollution.	A four-star project will show one or two ways to reduce garbage or pollution.	A five-star project will help you reduce garbage and pollution and actively protect the environment in many different ways.

Convert a Container into a Garden

Make space to grow your own food

Living Green Rating

★★★★★

- Reduces the need to buy fresh vegetables, fruits, or herbs, so less environmental impact
- Reduces landfill, because the old trash can, flowerpots, and aluminum cans are reused instead of being thrown out

One way to live greener is to grow some of your own food. It is cheap, easy, and does not harm the environment. It also means that you don't need to buy as much food.

What You Need

- Container, such as an old garbage bin or a wooden crate
- Drill
- Small spade
- Tarpaulin
- Drainage material, such as stones, broken flowerpots, or crushed aluminum cans
- **Topsoil** from your garden
- Sand
- Compost
- Watering can or hose

Do not use the drill yourself. Ask an adult to drill the holes for you ⚠

What to Do

1. Decide where your garden will go. Most plants grow best in full sunlight, so position your container where it will get plenty of sunshine.

2. If you are using a container with a solid bottom, such as a crate, ask an adult to drill some holes in the bottom.

3. Put a layer of drainage material in the bottom of the container. The drainage layer should be at least 2 inches (5 centimeters) deep.

You don't need a large backyard for gardening. You can use an old container to create a small garden.

4. Spread out the tarpaulin. On top of it, mix together equal amounts of the topsoil, sand, and compost.

5. Make enough soil mix to fill the container about one foot (30 cm). If your container is more than 14 in. (35 cm) deep, make the drainage layer deeper and still only add one foot (30 cm) of soil mix.

6. Shovel the soil mix into the container and spread it evenly.

7. Water the soil mix thoroughly.

8. Your new container garden is ready for planting!

Green Tip

Use your container garden to grow:
• vegetables (see pages 18–19)
• fruits, such as strawberries or blueberries
• herbs, such as mint or rosemary

Go Shopping in Your Garden

Grow your own vegetables at home

Growing your own vegetables is a great way of reducing the environmental impact of the food you eat. Most people agree that homegrown vegetables taste better than store-bought ones, too.

Living Green Rating

★ ★ ★ ★

- Reduces the need to buy fresh vegetables, so less environmental impact
- Reduces landfill, because the yogurt containers are not thrown out as garbage

What You Need

- Packets of vegetable seeds
- Container garden (see pages 16–17)
- Garden fork or trowel
- Watering can or hose
- Popsicle sticks
- Pencil
- Bamboo stakes
- Yogurt containers
- Plastic garden netting
- Stones
- String

What to Do

1. Choose a vegetable to grow in your garden. The vegetables listed in the table on page 19 are easy to care for and can be grown from seeds sown in outdoor containers. Plant them at the time of year listed in the chart.

2. Follow the instructions on the packet and sow the seeds.

3. Use popsicle sticks to mark where you have sown the seeds. Write the kind of vegetable on each stick.

4. Water the soil thoroughly.

When you have your own garden, you can grow the vegetables that you like to eat!

5. To protect your seeds and crop from birds and cats, place bamboo stakes in each corner and put a yogurt container on top of each stake. Place plastic garden netting over the stakes. Hold down the netting edges with stones.

6. Every day:
• check the soil, and water it if it feels dry
• remove weeds
• check for pests, such as slugs and snails. Remove them or make a trap.

7. Beans and corn will need staking once they start to grow. Place a bamboo stake in the soil beside each plant and tie it to the stake to keep it straight.

8. When ready, pick your vegetables, wash, cook, and eat!

What to Grow in Your Garden

Vegetables	When to Sow
Lettuce, radishes	All year round, depending on variety
Beans	Spring
Garden beet	Spring or summer
Corn, zucchini	Late spring or early summer
Spinach, carrots	Spring, summer, or fall

Green Tip

To improve the Living Green rating of this project:
• get rid of slugs using a **nontoxic** trap (see pages 20–21)
• water your garden with water that you collect in the shower
• use old lace curtains instead of plastic netting

A Trap for Hungry Slugs

Protect your food garden from pests

Slugs can cause a lot of damage to your plants in a short period of time. A sugar and yeast slug trap is a safe, environmentally friendly alternative to poisonous slug pellets. The trap does not poison slugs, it drowns them.

What You Need

• Used plastic container, such as a margarine tub
• Garden fork or trowel
• Large glass jar with lid
• 2 cups warm water
• A small packet of dry yeast
• 1 tablespoon salt
• 1 tablespoon sugar

What to Do

1. Wash and dry the plastic container.

2. Decide where you want the slug trap to go. It should be placed as close as possible to the plants you want to protect.

3. Using the trowel, dig a hole in the soil. The hole should be shallower than the container, so that about 1 inch (3 cm) of the container pokes up above the surface of the soil. This should prevent other, garden-friendly animals from falling into the hole by accident.

Slugs in your garden will be attracted to the smell of sugar and yeast working together in the trap.

4. Place the warm water, yeast, salt, and sugar in the glass jar. Put on the lid and shake the jar to mix.

5. Half-fill the plastic container with the mixture.

6. Check the trap every day and get rid of the drowned slugs.

7. Every few days, replace the yeast and sugar mixture.

Chili and Garlic Spray

Control pests with a nontoxic spray

A chili and garlic spray is an environmentally friendly way of getting rid of insect pests in your garden. It does not kill the pests, but it does a great job of keeping them away from your vegetables.

Living Green Rating

★ ★ ★ ★ ★

- Uses natural ingredients, so no toxic chemicals are released to pollute the environment
- Reduces landfill, because the old spray bottle is not thrown out as garbage

What You Need

- Chopping board
- Knife
- 10 garlic cloves
- 1 tablespoon vegetable oil
- 5 chilies
- 0.5 gallon (2 liters) boiling water
- Large bowl
- Wooden spoon
- Bar of soap
- Grater
- One-quarter cup warm water
- Large airtight container with lid
- Permanent marker
- Funnel
- Old spray bottle, emptied and cleaned
- Kitchen gloves (for chopping chilies)
- Garden gloves (for spraying)

What to Do

1. Peel and crush the garlic cloves.

2. Soak the crushed garlic in the vegetable oil for two days.

3. Finely chop the chilies.

Chilies can burn. Wear gloves and wash your hands thoroughly after handling the chilies or using the spray. Be careful not to get any in your eyes or in any cuts on your skin !

4. In a large bowl, combine the garlic mixture with the chopped chilies and the boiling water. Stir well.

Only use boiling water under adult supervision !

You don't have to kill pests to stop them from causing damage to your food plants. Keep them away with chilli and garlic spray!

5. Grate the bar of soap until you have 2 tablespoons of grated soap.

6. Dissolve the grated soap in the warm water.

7. Add the soap mixture to the bowl. Mix well.

8. Leave to cool and then pour into a large, airtight container with a lid.

9. Label the container and store it in a cool, dark place, out of reach of babies and small children. The mixture will keep for up to two months.

10. When you want to use the mixture, use a funnel to pour some into a spray bottle. Spray the food plants in your garden. For best results, use the spray regularly.

Green Tip

You can use your chili and garlic spray to keep cats and dogs from digging up your garden. The chili won't hurt your pets, but their sensitive noses will not like it!

Make a Solar Oven

Heat and cook food using the sun

A solar oven works by collecting the sun's rays and reflecting them into the oven. A sheet of clear plastic stops heat from escaping. Solar ovens are a green way of cooking food, because they use energy from the sun, called solar energy, which is a renewable resource.

What You Need

• Large pizza box
• Ruler
• Marker pen
• Scissors
• About 1.5 feet (50 cm) thin black cardboard
• About 3 feet (1 meter) aluminum foil
• About 1.5 feet (50 cm) clear plastic sheeting
• Duct tape
• Wood glue
• A 1-foot (30 cm) wooden dowel
• Food you want to heat or cook (see table on page 25)

What to Do

1. Draw a square on the lid of the pizza box, 0.8 inches (2 cm) in from each edge.

2. Cut along three sides of the square, and then fold along the fourth side to make a flap.

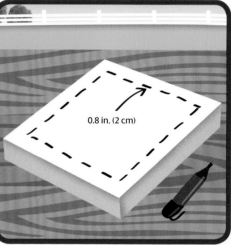

0.8 in. (2 cm)

aluminum foil

3. Cut a piece of aluminum foil to cover this flap. Glue it in place.

Don't throw away an old pizza box! Use it to cook your own food.

24

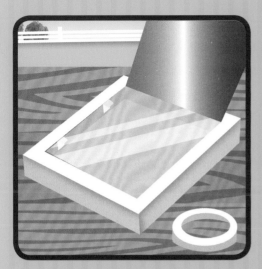

4. Cut the piece of clear plastic so that it fits snugly over the hole in the lid. Tape it to the underside of the lid.

5. Cut another piece of aluminum foil to fit inside the bottom of the box. Glue it in place.

Food You Can Heat in a Solar Oven

Food	Notes
Hot Dogs	Heat precooked hot dogs
Cookies	Bake until cookie dough is cooked
Pizzas	See pages 26–27
Chocolate and marshmallows	Place in paper cases and remove when gooey

6. Cut a piece of thin black cardboard that fits inside the bottom of the box. Glue it on top of the foil.

7. On a sunny day, put the solar oven outdoors in a place where it will receive plenty of sunlight. Face the flap toward the sun and prop it up with a piece of wooden dowel. Adjust the flap so that the maximum amount of sunlight is reflected into the oven.

8. Put your food in the oven. Eat when hot!

Homegrown Pizza

Make a tasty pizza using fresh, local ingredients

Using fresh, locally grown food that is in season is a good way to reduce the environmental impact of the food you eat. This pizza recipe uses whatever herbs and vegetables are in season.

Living Green Rating

★ ★ ★ ★

• Does not use food that has been imported or transported a long way, so less environmental impact

What You Need

- Store-bought pizza dough (or make your own using a recipe)
- Olive oil
- Baking tray
- 2 tablespoons tomato paste
- Block of mozzarella cheese
- Grater
- Cutting block
- Knife
- Fresh, locally grown vegetables that are in season
- Fresh, locally grown herbs that are in season
- Pastry brush
- Oven gloves
- Pizza cutter or knife

What to Do

1. If you are making your own pizza dough, follow the instructions in the recipe.

2. Preheat the oven to 450°F (230°C).

3. Lightly brush a baking tray with olive oil. Place the pizza dough on it.

4. Spread tomato paste evenly over the dough.

5. Grate half a cup of mozzarella and sprinkle half over the dough.

When you make your own pizza, you can make it the way you like it. You can use mozzarella cheese and add vegetables or herbs from your own garden.

6. Chop up the vegetables you are using as toppings and add them to the pizza.

7. Sprinkle the rest of the cheese over the toppings.

8. Tear up some fresh herbs and scatter them over the pizza.

9. Put the pizza in the oven and bake for twelve to fifteen minutes.

10. Take the pizza out of the oven using a pair of oven mitts.

Ask an adult for help when taking the pizza out of the oven ⚠

11. Cut the pizza into slices and enjoy!

Green Tip

To improve this project's Living Green rating, try cooking your pizza in a solar oven (see pages 24–55). You may need to double the cooking time.

Living Green Projects

Living Green Rating

★ ★ ★ ★

- Does not use food that has been imported or transported a long way, so less environmental impact

What You Need

- Wooden skewers
- Scissors
- Fresh, seasonal, locally grown fruit
- Knife
- Chopping block
- Small cookie cutter (optional)
- 1 cup plain yogurt
- 3 tablespoons honey
- Plate
- Small bowl

Fresh Fruit Kebabs

Make a tasty dessert using fresh, local fruit

Many desserts are unsustainable because they are highly processed, heavily packaged, and contain imported ingredients. These kebabs are a sustainable choice for dessert because they are made with locally grown, seasonal fruit — and they're delicious!

What to Do

1. Choose fruit for your kebabs. Choose a variety of colors and choose fairly firm fruit that will stay on the skewers, such as strawberries.

2. Depending on the types of fruit you are using, either wash or peel the fruit.

3. Chop the fruit into bite-sized pieces or cut out pieces using a cookie cutter.

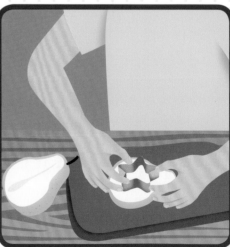

Choose fruit in a mixture of colors. Aim for four or more different colors.

4. Carefully cut off the sharp ends of the skewers with a pair of scissors.

5. Arrange the fruit pieces on the skewers.

6. Make a dip by stirring together the honey and yogurt in a small bowl.

7. Serve the kebabs on a plate, with the honey and yogurt dip beside them. Enjoy!

Green Tip

To improve the Living Green rating of this project:
• choose organic fruit
• make your own yogurt
• use locally produced honey
• collect the water that you used to wash the fruit, and water your garden with it

Find Out More About Living Green

The Internet is a great way of finding out more about how your food choices affect the environment and what you can do to eat more sustainably.

Useful Websites

Visit these useful websites:

 http://ecoguru.panda.org
Answer questions about the food you eat and other parts of your life and this calculator will let you know the sustainability of your lifestyle.

 www.thekidsgarden.co.uk
This gardening website for children and their parents has lots of gardening information, including tips on making compost and growing fruit and vegetables.

 http://unep.org/tunza/children
This website from the United Nations has downloadable fact sheets about environmental issues, tips for living more sustainably, and competitions you can enter.

Searching for Information

Here are some terms you might enter into your Internet search bar to find out more about food production and the environment:
- food processing
- sustainable agriculture
- organic gardening
- food miles

Glossary

algal bloom A sudden increase in the amount of algae growing in a body of water.

bacteria Microscopic living things, each of which is made up of a single cell.

carbon dioxide A greenhouse gas that is released when fossil fuels are burned, for example when coal is burned to make electricity.

environment The natural world, including plants, animals, land, rivers, and oceans.

export Send to another country for sale.

fertilize Add substances to the soil to help crops grow better.

fossil fuels Coal, oil, and natural gas, which are natural resources that are formed from the remains of dead plants and animals, deep under Earth's surface, over millions of years.

fungi (Plural of fungus) A group of living things that includes molds, yeast, mushrooms, and toadstools.

global warming The process by which Earth's average temperature is getting warmer.

greenhouse gas A gas, such as carbon dioxide or water vapor, that traps the heat of the sun in Earth's atmosphere.

habitat Place where plants and animals live.

imported Brought in from another country.

irrigated Supplied water to a dry area to help crops grow.

landfill Garbage that is buried and covered with soil at garbage dumps.

natural resources Natural materials that can be used by people, such as wood, metal, coal, and water.

nonrenewable resources Natural resources that cannot be easily replaced, such as coal, oil, and natural gas.

nontoxic Not poisonous to living things.

nutrients Substances that plants need in order to grow well.

organic Grown and produced without using artificial chemicals.

overfished Caught in very high numbers, meaning that the population of that fish is at risk.

pesticides Poisonous chemicals used to prevent pests, such as insects, fungi, and weeds, from damaging crops by killing pests.

pollution Damaging substances, especially chemicals or waste products, that harm the environment.

recycled Having treated the materials contained in a product so that they can be used again.

renewable resources Natural resources that will never run out, such as the wind, or that can easily be replaced, such as wood.

topsoil The top layer of soil, around 2–8 inches (5–20 cm) deep.

toxic Poisonous to living things.

Index